CREATION

In relation to end time, science, and evolution

Joshua O. Olumoye

Table of Contents

DEDICATION

This book is dedicated to God the Father, God the Son and God the Holy Spirit.

ACKNOWLEDGEMENTS

I hereby use this page to acknowledge all the people whom God have use to prepare me for the ministry.

I acknowledge all the men of God whom God uses to pray for me day and night, I pray your labor of love will never be in vain. Also, I thank my family and loved one for their prayer and support.

Finally, I acknowledge the God Almighty whom through the Holy Spirit keep and guide me into all things.

INTRODUCTION

CREATION

(In relation to end time, science, and evolution)

This book is a simple introduction to the creation in relation to the end time, science, and evolution.

This book is not a prophecy but just an assumption based on the bible 1 day to 1000 years theory.

There is a mystery behind the seven days creation of the heaven and earth.

Genesis 1:1-5

1 In the beginning God created the heaven and the earth.

2 And the earth was without form, and void; and darkness was upon the face of the deep. And the Spirit of God moved upon the face of the waters.

3 And God said, Let there be light: and there was light.

4 And God saw the light, that it was good: and God divided the light from the darkness.

5 And God called the light Day, and the darkness he called Night. And the evening and the morning were the first day.

Before I continue, I want you to know the heaven in this scripture is not the heaven the abode of God, heaven the abode of God is perfect.

Matthew 5:48

48 Be ye therefore perfect, even as your Father which is in heaven is perfect.

But this is the heaven below or rather the planets, the skies, and galaxies of this earth.

This is the same heaven and earth that will be renewed in the last day to get rid of the unrighteous, the demons and the fallen angels.

Isaiah 65:17

17 For, behold, I create new heavens and a new earth: and the former shall not be remembered, nor come into mind.

Revelation 21:1

1 And I saw a new heaven and a new earth: for the first heaven and the first earth were passed away; and there was no more sea.

Back to the seven days creation. The bible reveals hidden secrets in relationship between the creation and the time frame of the word of God.

These secrets are hidden but with the help of the Holy Spirits, studying and researching you get a clear and better understanding of the bible.

Bible said God through his words shows the end from the beginning, so we have to pay attention to the word of God.

Isaiah 46:10

10 Declaring the end from the beginning, and from ancient times the things that are not yet done, saying, My counsel shall stand, and I will do all my pleasure:

The word of God said 1 day is a thousand years to God.

2 Peter 3:8

8 But, beloved, be not ignorant of this one thing, that one day is with the Lord as a thousand years, and a thousand years as one day.

Psalm 90:4

4 For a thousand years in thy sight are but as yesterday when it is past, and as a watch in the night.

From this statement and from several revelations in the bible which you will see as you are reading this book there is a very strong indication that the end of this present evil world will come by the end of 6000 years.

God created the heaven and earth for six day and God rested from all his work in the 7 days.

Genesis 2:1-2

1 Thus the heavens and the earth were finished, and all the host of them.

2 And on the seventh day God ended his work which he had made; and he rested on the seventh day from all his work which he had made.

The bible said that in the last day Messiah will come and gathered the elects from the four corners of the world and they will reign with him for 1000 years.

Revelation 20:4-6

4 And I saw thrones, and they sat upon them, and judgment was given unto them: and I saw the souls of them that were beheaded for the witness of Jesus, and for the word of God, and which had not worshipped the beast, neither his image, neither had received his mark upon their foreheads, or in their hands; and they lived and reigned with Christ a thousand years.

5 But the rest of the dead lived not again until the thousand years were finished. This is the first resurrection.

6 Blessed and holy is he that hath part in the first resurrection: on such the second death hath no power, but they shall be priests of God and of Christ, and shall reign with him a thousand years.

This is confirming the seventh day rest of God and confirming that one day is 1000 years to God.

There is also a relationship between the creation and science. Science is the physical manifestation of the knowledge of Satan and this knowledge is a fragment of the heavenly knowledge and is set to oppose Godly knowledge and pervert humanity.

1 Timothy 6:20-21

20 O Timothy, keep that which is committed to thy trust, avoiding profane and vain babblings, and oppositions of science falsely so called:

21 Which some professing have erred concerning the faith. Grace be with thee. Amen.

Nevertheless, God's knowledge is incomparable, this was reflected in Daniel comparisons to the Babylonian scientist.

Daniel 1:4

4 Children in whom was no blemish, but well favoured, and skilful in all wisdom, and cunning in knowledge, and understanding science, and such as had ability in them to stand in the king's palace, and whom they might teach the learning and the tongue of the Chaldeans.

Daniel came out ten times better.

Daniel 1:20

20 And in all matters of wisdom and understanding, that the king enquired of them, he found them ten times better than all the magicians and astrologers that were in all his realm.

God cannot be proof, 1 day is 1000 years is not science. There is no searching of his understanding and knowledge.

Isaiah 40:28

28 Hast thou not known? hast thou not heard, that the everlasting God, the Lord, the Creator of the ends of the earth, fainteth not, neither is weary? there is no searching of his understanding.

The radioactive dating said the earth is 4.5 billion and bible said the earth is 6022 years, but they forget to realize that 1 day of God can be 4.5 million years of Satan or of science and technologies.

Science is the high thing that the bible say will exalt itself against the knowledge of God which we must always and regularly cast down.

2 Corinthians 10:4-5

4 (For the weapons of our warfare are not carnal, but mighty through God to the pulling down of strong holds;)

5 Casting down imaginations, and every high thing that exalteth itself against the knowledge of God, and bringing into captivity every thought to the obedience of Christ;

Finally, evolution is another thing that is here to disprove God. Evolution is the idea that came from Satan himself; this is Satan versus God. He is the beast that hates human that were made in the image of God.

Evolution is brought to negate the idea of creation and to say that there is no God, unknowingly to them evolution itself is a theory that cannot stand without creation.

CHAPTER 1

BIBLE

Before we go into the major topic let us briefly see the Bible so we can understand this topic better.

ON ITS OWN THE BIBLE IS LIMITED

Reading bible without the help of the HOLY SPIRIT or SATANIC backup for manipulations is like reading a story. Every word, sentences, verses, chapters in the Bible are outlines of a bigger thing to come, an outline to what God is doing and will do and, about what will eventually be the end of Satan. So, Bible is a shadow of things to come.

Colossians 2:16-17

16 Let no man therefore judge you in meat, or in drink, or in respect of an holyday, or of the new moon, or of the sabbath days:

17 Which are a shadow of things to come; but the body is of Christ.

The moment you open your bible to study, two kingdom is affected. First the kingdom of God knows that somebody is learning about YAHWEH and will send assistant to help you understand it better.

Acts 8:26-39

26 And the angel of the Lord spake unto Philip, saying, Arise, and go toward the south unto the way that goeth down from Jerusalem unto Gaza, which is desert.

27 And he arose and went: and, behold, a man of Ethiopia, an eunuch of great authority under Candace queen of the Ethiopians, who had the charge of all her treasure, and had come to Jerusalem for to worship,

28 Was returning, and sitting in his chariot read Esaias the prophet.

29 Then the Spirit said unto Philip, Go near, and join thyself to this chariot.

30 And Philip ran thither to him, and heard him read the prophet Esaias, and said, Understandest thou what thou readest?

31 And he said, How can I, except some man should guide me? And he desired Philip that he would come up and sit with him.

32 The place of the scripture which he read was this, He was led as a sheep to the slaughter; and like a lamb dumb before his shearer, so opened he not his mouth:

33 In his humiliation his judgment was taken away: and who shall declare his generation? for his life is taken from the earth.

34 And the eunuch answered Philip, and said, I pray thee, of whom speaketh the prophet this? of himself, or of some other man?

35 Then Philip opened his mouth, and began at the same scripture, and preached unto him Yeshua.

36 And as they went on their way, they came unto a certain water: and the eunuch said, See, here is water; what doth hinder me to be baptized?

37 And Philip said, If thou believest with all thine heart, thou mayest. And he answered and said, I believe that Yeshua Christ is the Son of God.

38 And he commanded the chariot to stand still: and they went down both into the water, both Philip and the eunuch; and he baptized him.

39 And when they were come up out of the water, the Spirit of the Lord caught away Philip, that the eunuch saw him no more: and he went on his way rejoicing.

At the same time the kingdom of darkness will be doing his best to discourage you, in order to keep you from knowing YAHWEH and know the truth about Satan.

The truth about Satan is that in Yeshua HaMashiach, you will overcome him. He doesn't want you to see scriptures about his weakness. For examples.

2 Corinthians 2:11

11 Lest Satan should get an advantage of us: for we are not ignorant of his devices.

James 4:7

7 Submit yourselves therefore to God. Resist the devil, and he will flee from you.

Philippians 4:13

13 I can do all things through Christ which strengtheneth me.

CANONIZATION, MANIPULATIONS AND CORRUPTION

Bible is the word of God, but the contents and packaging of the Bible were not put together by God but by a set of authorities.

CANONIZATION

A biblical canon, also called canon of scripture, is a set of books which a particular Jewish or Christian religious community regards as authoritative scriptures.

Canonization was a long process over time, the books that were deemed authentic and authoritative were included in the canon and the rest were discarded. These processes have developed through debate and agreement on the part of the religious authorities of their respective faiths and denominations. Some books have been excluded from various canons altogether, but many disputed books are considered by different groups to be biblical apocrypha (hidden or secret books) or deuterocanonical (books consider by Catholics, Eastern Orthodox and Assyrian churches as canonical books of the Old Testament) or pseudepigrapha (false author) by many, while some denominations may consider them fully canonical. Differences exist between the Hebrew Bible and Christian biblical canons, although most manuscripts are shared.

It's important to know that different religious groups include different books in their biblical canons. Most Protestant Bibles have 66 books. The Roman Catholic Bible has 73 books including the seven knowns as the Apocrypha. And the Ethiopian Orthodox Church have 81 books including pseudepigrapha like book of Enoch and Jubilees.

CRITERIA FOR CANONIZATION

There were hundreds of texts like those found in the New Testament and Old Testament that didn't make it into the canon. Such as Apocalypse of Peter, the Epistle of Barnabas, the Gospel of Thomas, The gospel of Mary, The gospel of Judas, Book of Enoch and more.

Why did some books make it, and others did not? This is based on criteria set by the canons. Three major criteria were as follows.

1 AUTHORSHIP: The author must be a prophet of God, an apostle or by someone close to them.

2 ACCEPTANCES: The text must come with establish weight of approval from those who were around when it was written.

3 CONNECTIONS: There must be a relationship or references between the text and other text in the canon or the text must be in line or build upon other text in the canon.

MANIPULATION AND CORRUPTION

Manipulation and corruption of the Bible was an Agenda of Satan. Bible canonization was done by the Gentiles without regarding the Jews.

Christianity was widely accepted by majority of faithful Gentiles, but it was taken over by their leaders and manipulated in order to fulfill the agenda of Antichrist.

For example, the book of Enoch and other books of the New Testament pass the criteria for canonization but was removed from the final compilation.

As we can see, Jude one of the inspired writers of the Bible quote directly from that book in the scriptures. Jude is a brother of James, and he was the writer of the book of Jude.

Jude 14-15

14 And Enoch also, the seventh from Adam, prophesied of these, saying, Behold, the Lord cometh with ten thousands of his saints,

15 To execute judgment upon all, and to convince all that are ungodly among them of all their ungodly deeds which they have ungodly committed, and of all their hard speeches which ungodly sinners have spoken against him.

This quotation was found in Enoch 1:9

Enoch 1:9

9 And behold! He cometh with ten thousands of His holy ones to execute judgement upon all, and to destroy all the ungodly, and will convict all flesh of all that the sinners and ungodly have wrought and ungodly committed against Him.

And the Bible himself told us little about Enoch and this little is big enough to know who Enoch was. A friend of God, God so loved him that he did not die, God just took him. He entered heaven alive.

Genesis 5:24

24 And Enoch walked with God: and he was not; for God took him.

So, we all see that this man was righteous. What disqualified the book of Enoch is very unclear, the book pass most of the criteria of canon, for example "another author of the Bible must quote from your book" and he was mentioned in Genesis. I believe his book was removed simply because of the deep secret about the mystery of eternal secrets which was the basis of paganism and witchcrafts.

Bible is a translation of translations; the Old Testament was written originally in Hebrews and that makes it more authentic but the New Testament which was written in Greek is more corrupt.

For Satan to achieve his desire soon the Bible is being revised more and more to suit his purpose.

NEW WORLD BIBLE

The new world Bible is an idea to take the true Christ from the church without you knowing it. This is going to be achieved by all this revised edition of the Bible.

2 Thessalonians 2:7 (KJV)

7 For the mystery of iniquity doth already work: only he who now letteth will let, until he be taken out of the way.

Here Bible tells us that the work of Antichrist is at work already, but the full manifestation will not come until Christ is taken out of way.

King James version of the Bible was the only edition that was revised closely from the original manuscript. Printed in 1611, authorize by King James, translated by 54 scholars divided into group of six, it took them 7 years to complete.

All the revised editions claim King James is difficult to understand so they decide to make it simple. These changes are calculated to attack specific doctrines of the Bible, they are not accidental.

NIV is the most popular and is missing 16 entire verses from the New Testament.

Compare these scriptures.

Time of reformation changed to new order.

Hebrews 9:10 (KJV)

10 Which stood only in meats and drinks, and divers washings, and carnal ordinances, imposed on them until the time of reformation.

Hebrews 9:10 (NIV)

10 They are only a matter of food and drink and various ceremonial washings—external regulations applying until the time of the new order.

The prove of trinity is remove from NIV.

1 John 5:7 (KJV)

7 For there are three that bear record in heaven, the Father, the Word, and the Holy Ghost: and these three are one.

1 John 5:7(NIV)

7 For there are three that testify:

What about this miss up?

Isaiah 14:12 (KJV)

12 How art thou fallen from heaven, O Lucifer, son of the morning! how art thou cut down to the ground, which didst weaken the nations!

Lucifer here is Son of the morning.

Now look at Revelations 22

Revelation 22:16 (KJV)

16 I Yeshua have sent mine angel to testify unto you these things in the churches. I am the root and the offspring of David, and the bright and morning star.

Yeshua here is the bright and morning star.

Now Isaiah 14:12 NIV has replaced the title of lucifer with the title of Yeshua.

Isaiah 14:12 (NIV)

12 How you have fallen from heaven, morning star, son of the dawn! You have been cast down to the earth, you who once laid low the nations!

So, in the future they are going to tell you Yeshua was the one that was cast out of heaven.

NEW KING JAMES VERSION

The new king James is one of the most dangerous versions out there. They realize people are running from some translation they now said let us call it new king James version, so you think is the same.

The new king James omits the word Lords 66 times, God 51 times. Heaven 50 times repent 44 times, the blood 23 times, hell 22 times.

Completely remove the world Jehovah, Damnation, the term New Testament and the word devil and they secretly change some words that you will never notice unless the Holy Spirit shows you.

Compare these two scriptures.

1 Corinthians 1:18 (KJV)

18 For the preaching of the cross is to them that perish foolishness; but unto us which are saved it is the power of God.

1 Corinthians 1:18 (NKJV)

18 For the [a1]message of the cross is foolishness to those who are perishing, but to us who are being saved it is the power of God.

Do you see the different 'that are saved" but in NKJV it says "being saved" as if it were a process. No, the moment you give your life to Yeshua you are saved.

The people behind all this version were all antichrists. The aim is to disarm you of your weapon. When the word is diluted, it will be of known effect.

Mark 7:13 (KJV)

13 Making the word of God of none effect through your tradition, which ye have delivered: and many such like things do ye.

---

1.   *https://www.biblegateway.com/*

passage/?search=1+Corinthians+1%3A18&version=NKJV#fen-NKJV-28382a

The aim is to take sharp two-edged sword from you and give you dull non effective one.

Hebrews 4:12 (KJV)

12 For the word of God is quick, and powerful, and sharper than any twoedged sword, piercing even to the dividing asunder of soul and spirit, and of the joints and marrow, and is a discerner of the thoughts and intents of the heart.

THE BIBLE IS STILL SOLID

The good news is that upon all the manipulation and corruptions the Bible is still more than enough to accomplish your heavenly journey. Everything that was added or taken out was not behind God. God is the author of the Bible and whatever we have is still the word of God.

2 Timothy 3:16-17

16 All scripture is given by inspiration of God, and is profitable for doctrine, for reproof, for correction, for instruction in righteousness:

17 That the man of God may be perfect, thoroughly furnished unto all good works.

2 Peter 1:20-21

20 Knowing this first, that no prophecy of the scripture is of any private interpretation.

21 For the prophecy came not in old time by the will of man: but holy men of God spake as they were moved by the Holy Ghost.

The above two scriptures let us know that the scriptures are inspired by God and not by man.

Like I have early said Bible is an outline of a bigger things to come, not everything can be written but everything can be revealed.

John 20:30-31

30 And many other signs truly did Yeshua in the presence of his disciples, which are not written in this book:

31 But these are written, that ye might believe that Yeshua is the Christ, the Son of God; and that believing ye might have life through his name.

What is John telling us here? He said not everything was recorded, but what we have today is mor than enough to bring us to a saving faith.

By studying the Bible all secret will be revealed to you with the help of Holy Spirit.

Luke 8:17

17 For nothing is secret, that shall not be made manifest; neither any thing hid, that shall not be known and come abroad.

Luke 12:2

2 For there is nothing covered, that shall not be revealed; neither hid, that shall not be known.

CHAPTER 2

CHAOTIC WORLD

THE WORLD BEFORE MAN

Chaotic world is a time when the world was in total confusion or lack of order, that is "form and void" and that was the situation of the world in Genesis 1:2

Genesis 1:2

2 And the earth was without form, and void; and darkness was upon the face of the deep. And the Spirit of God moved upon the face of the waters.

And to understand this better we must comb the scriptures from the beginning to the end.

ALL SCRIPTIURES WORKS TOGETHER

While studying the Bible I realize that scriptures comprehend themselves. For you to grasp little idea about the word of God you have to read the whole scriptures. There are things you will read in the book of Genesis that you will not understand very well until you see its better explanations in another scripture.

For example, John 1:1-5 let us know that Genesis 1:1 is not the actual beginning, that there was a beginning before the beginning and other scriptures shows that there is a gap between Genesis 1:1 and Genesis 1:2.

This is why we need to study; I mean study always.

2 Timothy 2:15

15 Study to shew thyself approved unto God, a workman that needeth not to be ashamed, rightly dividing the word of truth.

God does not usually explain all there is to know about a subject in one place in the Bible.

Even his prophets and the writers He inspired did not always fully understand what they recorded but they write whatever is revealed by God.

Daniel 12:8-9

8 And I heard, but I understood not: then said I, O my Lord, what shall be the end of these things?

9 And he said, Go thy way, Daniel: for the words are closed up and sealed till the time of the end.

Even Paul made it clear that our knowledge and prophecy are not completely accurate because we only know in part and prophecy in part. Only God is accurate.

1 Corinthians 13:9

9 For we know in part, and we prophesy in part.

You have to join all the parts together to make it whole. And this explains the gap theory.

THE EARTH, AND PRE-ADAMIC BEINGS

The Lord made the earth different from heaven and from all other planets, a place where spiritual things will be made visible in the physical.

THE WORLD BEFORE MAN

Genesis 1:1-2

1 In the beginning God created the heaven and the earth.

2 And the earth was without form, and void; and darkness was upon the face of the deep. And the Spirit of God moved upon the face of the waters.

According to the above scripture there is a possibility of life in this earth that were destroyed before the creation of Adam and Eve.

To understand this better we must comb the scriptures from the beginning to the end.

ALL SCRIPTIURES WORKS TOGETHER

While studying the Bible I realize that scriptures comprehend themselves. For you to grasp little idea about the word of God you have to read the whole scriptures. There are things you will read in the book of Genesis that you will not understand very well until you see its better explanations in another scripture.

For example, John 1:1-5 let us know that Genesis 1:1 is not the actual beginning, that there was a beginning before the beginning and other scriptures shows that there is a gap between Genesis 1:1 and Genesis 1:2.

This is why we need to study; I mean study always.

2 Timothy 2:15

15 Study to shew thyself approved unto God, a workman that needeth not to be ashamed, rightly dividing the word of truth.

God does not usually explain all there is to know about a subject in one place in the Bible. Even his prophets and the writers He inspired did not always fully understand what they recorded.

Daniel 12:8-9

8 And I heard, but I understood not: then said I, O my Lord, what shall be the end of these things?

9 And he said, Go thy way, Daniel: for the words are closed up and sealed till the time of the end.

Even Paul made it clear that our knowledge and prophecy are not completely accurate because we only know in part and prophecy in part. Only God is accurate.

1 Corinthians 13:9

9 For we know in part, and we prophesy in part.

You have to join all the parts together to make it whole. And this explains the gap theory.

THE GAP THEORY

The gap theorist believes there is a gap between Genesis 1:1 and Genesis 1:2. I too believe there is possibility of gap between those verses. Base on the section above where I was talking about scriptures comprehend each other better explain the gap theory.

Consider, for example.

Genesis 1:1

1 In the beginning God created the heaven and the earth.

That was a beginning, let us consider another beginning.

John 1:1-3

1 In the beginning was the Word, and the Word was with God, and the Word was God.

2 The same was in the beginning with God.

3 All things were made by him; and without him was not any thing made that was made.

Now you will see that this was a beginning before the beginning in Genesis 1:1. Because John took us to the time before the creation, he took us to the creator himself. "All things were made by him; and without him was not anything made that was made." This information helps us understand who God was in the beginning and at the time of the earth's creation.

Paul makes the creator and the created clearer in the book of Colossians.

Colossians 1:15-17

15 Who is the image of the invisible God, the firstborn of every creature:

16 For by him were all things created, that are in heaven, and that are in earth, visible and invisible, whether they be thrones, or dominions, or principalities, or powers: all things were created by him, and for him:

17 And he is before all things, and by him all things consist.

Now we know that the divine word (Yeshua) was with God before the creation of heaven and the earth and God made everything through Him.

Similarly, Genesis 1:2 describes the earth as being "without form, and void."

Genesis 1:2

2 And the earth was without form, and void; and darkness was upon the face of the deep. And the Spirit of God moved upon the face of the waters.

Now, suddenly after the creation of Genesis 1:1 "the earth was without form and void; and darkness was upon the face of the deep." This verse does not really explain why the earth was in this condition. However, God reveals more details in other parts of His Word which we will see as we continue.

Something happened between the first two verses of Genesis to cause the earth to become desolate and uninhabitable after having been initially made perfect.

PRE-ADAMIC BEING AND REBELLIOUS

The archeologist and scientist believed that human-like creatures existed before Adam. And some Bible scholars believed they might be angelic being because the fossils that we find today testify to their existence.

Though they are different in nature to human being.

As per the decreasing in the level and powers of the angels from Seraphim to guardian angels in the ranks of angels I believed the initial inhabitant of the earth were the lowest rank of angels.

I believe these angels were corrupted and rebellious and that there was a judgement on the rebellion and the judgement was flood according to Genesis 1:2 (b) *"And the Spirit of God moved upon the face of the waters."*

And according to Isaiah 24:1 the earth was inhabited before the Lord make it empty and it becomes forms and void.

Isaiah 24:1

1 Behold, the Lord maketh the earth empty, and maketh it waste, and turneth it upside down, and scattereth abroad the inhabitants thereof.

He "scattereth abroad the inhabitants thereof." And that was the conditions of the earth as a result of judgement.

God further reveals more details in other parts of His Word again about 'form and void and darkness."

Jeremiah 4:23-26

23 I beheld the earth, and, lo, it was without form, and void; and the heavens, and they had no light.

24 I beheld the mountains, and, lo, they trembled, and all the hills moved lightly.

25 I beheld, and, lo, there was no man, and all the birds of the heavens were fled.

26 I beheld, and, lo, the fruitful place was a wilderness, and all the cities thereof were broken down at the presence of the Lord, and by his fierce anger.

And Job talks about the creation and the angel rejoicing.

Job 38:4-7

4 Where wast thou when I laid the foundations of the earth? declare, if thou hast understanding.

5 Who hath laid the measures thereof, if thou knowest? or who hath stretched the line upon it?

6 Whereupon are the foundations thereof fastened? or who laid the corner stone thereof;

7 When the morning stars sang together, and all the sons of God shouted for joy?

The "morning stars" and "sons of God" these are angels including Lucifer (not yet cast down) rejoicing at the beauty of initial creations.

Another thing to consider, showing that there might be pre-Adamic being is the commandment given to Adam and Eve by God to replenish the earth. The meaning of replenish is to fill or build up again, you can only replenish something that has been before.

Genesis 1:28

28 And God blessed them, and God said unto them, Be fruitful, and multiply, and replenish the earth, and subdue it: and have dominion over the fish of the sea, and over the fowl of the air, and over every living thing that moveth upon the earth.

That same commandment was given to Noah after the flood.

Genesis 9:1

1 And God blessed Noah and his sons, and said unto them, Be fruitful, and multiply, and replenish the earth.

Fill it up again.

WHAT HAPPENED

Genesis 1:1

1 In the beginning God created the heaven and the earth.

According to this scripture the heaven and the earth created by God were perfect. God never create anything without form and void.

God is a master builder. Bible says God is not the author of confusion. That is God is not the creator of confusion.

1 Corinthians 14:33

33 For God is not the author of confusion, but of peace, as in all churches of the saints.

He is not the type that will say let us try this and see if it will work. In the beginning God created the heavens and the earth. Simple.

Genesis 1:2

2 And the earth was without form, and void; and darkness was upon the face of the deep. And the Spirit of God moved upon the face of the waters.

Verse 2 "And the earth was without form and void," I believe something happens, just like it happens in the days of Noah and as is going to happen in the last day war of Armageddon and God wiped the rebellious out. God knows the beginning from the end.

ANGELIC REVOLTS

Again, God reveals in his word that there was a great angel, Lucifer, who rebelled against Him, this is to confirm that the angel has been revolting from the beginning.

Isaiah 14:12-16

12 How art thou fallen from heaven, O Lucifer, son of the morning! how art thou cut down to the ground, which didst weaken the nations!

13 For thou hast said in thine heart, I will ascend into heaven, I will exalt my throne above the stars of God: I will sit also upon the mount of the congregation, in the sides of the north:

14 I will ascend above the heights of the clouds; I will be like the most High.

15 Yet thou shalt be brought down to hell, to the sides of the pit.

16 They that see thee shall narrowly look upon thee, and consider thee, saying, Is this the man that made the earth to tremble, that did shake kingdoms;

And this rebellion was further described in the book of revelations.

Revelation 12:7-9

7 And there was war in heaven: Michael and his angels fought against the dragon; and the dragon fought and his angels,

8 And prevailed not; neither was their place found any more in heaven.

9 And the great dragon was cast out, that old serpent, called the Devil, and Satan, which deceiveth the whole world: he was cast out into the earth, and his angels were cast out with him.

And we know this war was because of Yeshua HaMashiach because devil knew the whole plan of God is for Yeshua to reign as king in heaven and on earth. Which to Satan is a cheat, he believed he should be the one to get that position and not son of man. "I am the anointed cherub that covers," "I am the second in command". He rebelled and was able to convince one third of the angels to follow him.

Revelation 12:3-5

3 And there appeared another wonder in heaven; and behold a great red dragon, having seven heads and ten horns, and seven crowns upon his heads.

4 And his tail drew the third part of the stars of heaven, and did cast them to the earth: and the dragon stood before the woman which was ready to be delivered, for to devour her child as soon as it was born.

5 And she brought forth a man child, who was to rule all nations with a rod of iron: and her child was caught up unto God, and to his throne.

All these events took place in the spirit realm before the creation of Adam and Eve. Yeshua even testified that he saw Satan fell from heaven. That is, he is the word that was with God and witness everything as Satan fell.

Luke 10:18

18 And he said unto them, I beheld Satan as lightning fall from heaven.

Lucifer, who became Satan (meaning Adversary) at his rebellion, was cast down from heaven to the earth! And since then, retains his authority over this planet. Even the dominion that was meant for mankind was stolen from Adam by the same Satan.

No wonder Satan told Yeshua in the book of Luke chapter four that the earth was delivered unto him, and Yeshua did not disprove it. Bur Yeshua knew that that was what he came for. To take it back.

Luke 4:5-8

5 And the devil, taking him up into an high mountain, shewed unto him all the kingdoms of the world in a moment of time.

6 And the devil said unto him, All this power will I give thee, and the glory of them: for that is delivered unto me; and to whomsoever I will I give it.

7 If thou therefore wilt worship me, all shall be thine.

8 And Yeshua answered and said unto him, Get thee behind me, Satan: for it is written, Thou shalt worship the Lord thy God, and him only shalt thou serve.

Yeshua resisted the temptation but did not dispute the assertion of Satan's present authority. And that is why I come, I come to take over and the only way is to conquer sin on the cross and whosoever shall repent and call on my name shall be save from you Satan.

Satan is the ruler of this world no doubt.

John 14:30

30 Hereafter I will not talk much with you: for the prince of this world cometh, and hath nothing in me.

John 12:31

31 Now is the judgment of this world: now shall the prince of this world be cast out.

And Paul called him god of this world.

2 Corinthians 4:4

4 In whom the god of this world hath blinded the minds of them which believe not, lest the light of the glorious gospel of Christ, who is the image of God, should shine unto them.

The earth is Satan's realm. He moves about to and fro looking for whom to attack. That is why we are to be sober and be vigilant.

1 Peter 5:8

8 Be sober, be vigilant; because your adversary the devil, as a roaring lion, walketh about, seeking whom he may devour:

The book of Job confirms this when the Lord ask him "where are you coming from"?

Job 1:7

7 And the Lord said unto Satan, Whence comest thou? Then Satan answered the Lord, and said, From going to and fro in the earth, and from walking up and down in it.

You can see his answer "from going to and fro in the earth.

It is no accident that in Genesis 3, shortly after God created Adam and Eve, Satan appeared on the scene as the serpent in the garden for he has been casted down to the earth before man's creation took place.

SATAN DWELL IN EDEN BEFORE ADAM.

Ezekiel 28:13-19

13 Thou hast been in Eden the garden of God; every precious stone was thy covering, the sardius, topaz, and the diamond, the beryl, the onyx, and the jasper, the sapphire, the emerald, and the carbuncle, and gold: the workmanship of thy tabrets and of thy pipes was prepared in thee in the day that thou wast created.

14 Thou art the anointed cherub that covereth; and I have set thee so: thou wast upon the holy mountain of God; thou hast walked up and down in the midst of the stones of fire.

15 Thou wast perfect in thy ways from the day that thou wast created, till iniquity was found in thee.

16 By the multitude of thy merchandise they have filled the midst of thee with violence, and thou hast sinned: therefore I will cast thee as profane out of the mountain of God: and I will destroy thee, O covering cherub, from the midst of the stones of fire.

17 Thine heart was lifted up because of thy beauty, thou hast corrupted thy wisdom by reason of thy brightness: I will cast thee to the ground, I will lay thee before kings, that they may behold thee.

18 Thou hast defiled thy sanctuaries by the multitude of thine iniquities, by the iniquity of thy traffick; therefore will I bring forth a fire from the midst of thee, it shall devour thee, and I will bring thee to ashes upon the earth in the sight of all them that behold thee.

19 All they that know thee among the people shall be astonished at thee: thou shalt be a terror, and never shalt thou be any more.

The above passage speaks of Satan dwelling in Eden, the Garden of God, before sin had infected it and this is a description of the original perfection before God judged the world.

I believe all his violent dealing and trading were with Pre-Adamic beings.

THE EARTH WAS RENEWED OR RECREATED

According to David who was inspired by Holy Spirit to write Psalm 104:30

Psalm 104:30

30 Thou sendest forth thy spirit, they are created: and thou renewest the face of the earth.

And everything hidden is coming to surface gradually, eyes are opening, mystery are unfolding, science are discovering more things. Yeshua said every hidden thing will be revealed.

Mark 4:22

22 For there is nothing hid, which shall not be manifested; neither was anything kept secret, but that it should come abroad.

For the earth shall be filled with the knowledge of God.

Habakkuk 2:14

14 For the earth shall be filled with the knowledge of the glory of the Lord, as the waters cover the sea.

BIBLE AGES AND YEARS NOT IN AGREEMENT WITH SCIENCE.

The Bible and science are not in agreement in age of creations. The fossil record shows the world to be about a billion years old and adding up the ages of the biblical patriarchs yields a date of about 6,000 years ago for the first human parents, Adam, and Eve, formed by God at the end of six days of creation.

Well, there might be flaws in dating methods. We have to understand that God is not bound by time like human beings. He is everlasting.

Hebrews 13:8

8 Yeshua Christ the same yesterday, and to day, and for ever.

And the Bible says one day is with the Lord as a thousand years.

2 Peter 3:8

8 But, beloved, be not ignorant of this one thing, that one day is with the Lord as a thousand years, and a thousand years as one day.

And the psalmist said a thousand yeas is like yesterday to God.

Psalm 90:4

4 For a thousand years in thy sight are but as yesterday when it is past, and as a watch in the night.

Though looking at these verses we cannot conclude that it is a day of Genesis. Many considered this word to be a figure of speech, but I believe is a word of comparison. God did not just put those word there.

Did you know that God can and has used natural disaster in a supernatural way to impact the surface of the earth with thousands of years of change in only one day?

A volcanic eruption changes the surface of the earth in one day and the result is more than what the earth went through in a thousand years to achieve same result. So, when a fossil reads a thousand years, it does not change anything about God.

And look at what happens between Satan and Yeshua at the temptation of Yeshua Christ. He showed Yeshua all his limited glory in a space of time.

Luke 4:5

5 And the devil, taking him up into an high mountain, shewed unto him all the kingdoms of the world in a moment of time.

He showed him everything from beginning to the end "moment of time" is like a flash, but to those who are not limited by time they can see 1 million years of a thing in 1 moment.

CHAPTER 3

THE CREATION IN RELATION TO THE END TIME

In this chapter we will study Genesis chapter 1 and unlock the plans and mystery of the end time.

Bible let us know in Isaiah 46:10 that Yahweh has already declare the end from the beginning.

Isaiah 46:10

10 Declaring the end from the beginning, and from ancient times the things that are not yet done, saying, My counsel shall stand, and I will do all my pleasure:

So, everything about the world timeline is all in that Genesis chapter 1. Each day of creations represent a thousand years. And that is the same order in which the end will come.

Revelation 20 will shed more light on this, Satan will be bound for 1000 years, and we will reign with Yeshua for 100 years.

Revelation 20:2

2 And he laid hold on the dragon, that old serpent, which is the Devil, and Satan, and bound him a thousand years,

Revelation 20:6

6 Blessed and holy is he that hath part in the first resurrection: on such the second death hath no power, but they shall be priests of God and of Christ and shall reign with him a thousand years.

THE TIMELINE

Genesis 1

1 In the beginning God created the heaven and the earth.

2 And the earth was without form, and void; and darkness was upon the face of the deep. And the Spirit of God moved upon the face of the waters.

3 And God said, Let there be light: and there was light.

4 And God saw the light, that it was good: and God divided the light from the darkness.

5 And God called the light Day, and the darkness he called Night. And the evening and the morning were the first day.

6 And God said, Let there be a firmament in the midst of the waters, and let it divide the waters from the waters.

7 And God made the firmament, and divided the waters which were under the firmament from the waters which were above the firmament: and it was so.

8 And God called the firmament Heaven. And the evening and the morning were the second day.

9 And God said, Let the waters under the heaven be gathered together unto one place, and let the dry land appear: and it was so.

10 And God called the dry land Earth; and the gathering together of the waters called he Seas: and God saw that it was good.

11 And God said, Let the earth bring forth grass, the herb yielding seed, and the fruit tree yielding fruit after his kind, whose seed is in itself, upon the earth: and it was so.

12 And the earth brought forth grass, and herb yielding seed after his kind, and the tree yielding fruit, whose seed was in itself, after his kind: and God saw that it was good.

13 And the evening and the morning were the third day.

14 And God said, Let there be lights in the firmament of the heaven to divide the day from the night; and let them be for signs, and for seasons, and for days, and years:

15 And let them be for lights in the firmament of the heaven to give light upon the earth: and it was so.

16 And God made two great lights; the greater light to rule the day, and the lesser light to rule the night: he made the stars also.

17 And God set them in the firmament of the heaven to give light upon the earth,

18 And to rule over the day and over the night, and to divide the light from the darkness: and God saw that it was good.

19 And the evening and the morning were the fourth day.

20 *And God said, Let the waters bring forth abundantly the moving creature that hath life, and fowl that may fly above the earth in the open firmament of heaven.*

21 *And God created great whales, and every living creature that moveth, which the waters brought forth abundantly, after their kind, and every winged fowl after his kind: and God saw that it was good.*

22 *And God blessed them, saying, Be fruitful, and multiply, and fill the waters in the seas, and let fowl multiply in the earth.*

23 *And the evening and the morning were the fifth day.*

24 *And God said, Let the earth bring forth the living creature after his kind, cattle, and creeping thing, and beast of the earth after his kind: and it was so.*

25 *And God made the beast of the earth after his kind, and cattle after their kind, and every thing that creepeth upon the earth after his kind: and God saw that it was good.*

26 *And God said, Let us make man in our image, after our likeness: and let them have dominion over the fish of the sea, and over the fowl of the air, and over the cattle, and over all the earth, and over every creeping thing that creepeth upon the earth.*

27 *So God created man in his own image, in the image of God created he him; male and female created he them.*

28 *And God blessed them, and God said unto them, Be fruitful, and multiply, and replenish the earth, and subdue it: and have dominion over the fish of the sea, and over the fowl of the air, and over every living thing that moveth upon the earth.*

29 *And God said, Behold, I have given you every herb bearing seed, which is upon the face of all the earth, and every tree, in the which is the fruit of a tree yielding seed; to you it shall be for meat.*

30 *And to every beast of the earth, and to every fowl of the air, and to every thing that creepeth upon the earth, wherein there is life, I have given every green herb for meat: and it was so.*

31 And God saw every thing that he had made, and, behold, it was very good. And the evening and the morning were the sixth day.

From the above scripture we saw that Yahweh created everything in six days and on the seventh day he rested. Seven is God's number of perfections.

And each day of these seven days represent a thousand years and events that happens in these seven days from careful observations corresponds to the events that happens in the last 6000 years of creation.

2 Peter 3:8

8 But, beloved, be not ignorant of this one thing, that one day is with the Lord as a thousand years, and a thousand years as one day.

This will be clearer as we continue.

CHAPTER 4

DAY 1 FIRST MILLENNIUM EVENTS 4000-3000 BC

We will start from Genesis 1:1-5 which is the first day.

Genesis 1:1-5

1 In the beginning God created the heaven and the earth.

2 And the earth was without form, and void; and darkness was upon the face of the deep. And the Spirit of God moved upon the face of the waters.

3 And God said, Let there be light: and there was light.

4 And God saw the light, that it was good: and God divided the light from the darkness.

5 And God called the light Day, and the darkness he called Night. And the evening and the morning were the first day.

God created an environment where he will live and is creating a bride.

The son was in the beginning. He was the lamb that was slain from the foundation of the world.

The first thing that was created is light, "let there be light". Who is light? And the answer is Yeshua HaMashiach. John explains this better in John chapter 1.

John 1:1-5

1 In the beginning was the Word, and the Word was with God, and the Word was God.

2 The same was in the beginning with God.

3 All things were made by him; and without him was not any thing made that was made.

4 In him was life; and the life was the light of men.

5 And the light shineth in darkness; and the darkness comprehended it not.

And Yeshua confirms this in John 8:12

John 8:12

12 Then spake Yeshua again unto them, saying, I am the light of the world: he that followeth me shall not walk in darkness, but shall have the light of life.

Yeshua is the light, the light of life. What is life? Life is what makes us different from non-living things and this life is in the blood.

There is much hidden secret, in that first ever WORD spoken by ELOHIM "let there be light". In that word Yeshua was slain for the remission of mankind even at the foundation of the world.

The hidden truth here is found in Revelation 3:8

Revelation 13:8

8 And all that dwell upon the earth shall worship him, whose names are not written in the book of life of the Lamb slain from the foundation of the world.

The blood of Yeshua was shed for the sins of the world at the creation and this blood is the life of men, which was the light of men and also the light for the creation to be made possible.

For "All things were made by him; and without him was not any thing made that was made. In him was life; and the life was the light of men."

This mission became clear to mankind only after He had been crucified on the cross.

Peter repeats this truth in when he wrote about Yeshua as being foreordained.

1 Peter 1:20

20 Who verily was foreordained before the foundation of the world, but was manifest in these last times for you,

Even Satan did not know about this shed blood until Yeshua was crucified.

This light is not the sun moon or star, nor the cosmos, but this light is Yeshua which encompasses everything in the universe, life, visible and invincible lights.

Let us see the 1000 years events of day one creation.

Adam and Eve were beguiled, and Yahweh cursed them, and they died.

All the 1000 years story can be found in Genesis chapter 4.

Genesis 4

4 And Adam knew Eve his wife; and she conceived, and bare Cain, and said, I have gotten a man from the Lord.

2 And she again bare his brother Abel. And Abel was a keeper of sheep, but Cain was a tiller of the ground.

3 And in process of time it came to pass, that Cain brought of the fruit of the ground an offering unto the Lord.

4 And Abel, he also brought of the firstlings of his flock and of the fat thereof. And the Lord had respect unto Abel and to his offering:

5 But unto Cain and to his offering he had not respect. And Cain was very wroth, and his countenance fell.

6 And the Lord said unto Cain, Why art thou wroth? and why is thy countenance fallen?

7 If thou doest well, shalt thou not be accepted? and if thou doest not well, sin lieth at the door. And unto thee shall be his desire, and thou shalt rule over him.

8 And Cain talked with Abel his brother: and it came to pass, when they were in the field, that Cain rose up against Abel his brother, and slew him.

9 And the Lord said unto Cain, Where is Abel thy brother? And he said, I know not: Am I my brother's keeper?

10 And he said, What hast thou done? the voice of thy brother's blood crieth unto me from the ground.

11 And now art thou cursed from the earth, which hath opened her mouth to receive thy brother's blood from thy hand;

12 When thou tillest the ground, it shall not henceforth yield unto thee her strength; a fugitive and a vagabond shalt thou be in the earth.

13 And Cain said unto the Lord, My punishment is greater than I can bear.

14 Behold, thou hast driven me out this day from the face of the earth; and from thy face shall I be hid; and I shall be a fugitive and a vagabond in the earth; and it shall come to pass, that every one that findeth me shall slay me.

15 And the Lord said unto him, Therefore whosoever slayeth Cain, vengeance shall be taken on him sevenfold. And the Lord set a mark upon Cain, lest any finding him should kill him.

16 And Cain went out from the presence of the Lord, and dwelt in the land of Nod, on the east of Eden.

17 And Cain knew his wife; and she conceived, and bare Enoch: and he builded a city, and called the name of the city, after the name of his son, Enoch.

18 And unto Enoch was born Irad: and Irad begat Mehujael: and Mehujael begat Methusael: and Methusael begat Lamech.

19 And Lamech took unto him two wives: the name of the one was Adah, and the name of the other Zillah.

20 And Adah bare Jabal: he was the father of such as dwell in tents, and of such as have cattle.

21 And his brother's name was Jubal: he was the father of all such as handle the harp and organ.

22 And Zillah, she also bare Tubalcain, an instructer of every artificer in brass and iron: and the sister of Tubalcain was Naamah.

23 And Lamech said unto his wives, Adah and Zillah, Hear my voice; ye wives of Lamech, hearken unto my speech: for I have slain a man to my wounding, and a young man to my hurt.

24 If Cain shall be avenged sevenfold, truly Lamech seventy and sevenfold.

25 And Adam knew his wife again; and she bare a son, and called his name Seth: For God, said she, hath appointed me another seed instead of Abel, whom Cain slew.

26 And to Seth, to him also there was born a son; and he called his name Enos: then began men to call upon the name of the Lord.

In summary Adam knew his wife and Cain was born, and later Abel was born.

Here we see the first offering to God and the first murderer Cain.

Cain got married and his wife will be from among his sisters for this time bible did not record about female birth. But bible said Adam begat sons and daughters.

Genesis 5:4

4 And the days of Adam after he had begotten Seth were eight hundred years: and he begat sons and daughters:

Adam and Eve begat another son called Seth that took the place of the first son for Cain was no longer regarded as a true son and Seth begat Enos which begin again the worshiping of the Lord.

Adam died at the age of 930 years.

Genesis 5:5

5 And all the days that Adam lived were nine hundred and thirty years: and he died.

That was the first 1000 years.

CHAPTER 5

DAY 2 SECOND MILLENNIUM EVENTS 3000 – 2000 BC

Second day, beginning of civilization.

Genesis 1:6-8

6 And God said, Let there be a firmament in the midst of the waters, and let it divide the waters from the waters.

7 And God made the firmament, and divided the waters which were under the firmament from the waters which were above the firmament: and it was so.

8 And God called the firmament Heaven. And the evening and the morning were the second day.

Pay close attention to these scriptures you will find something that is in every other day that was missing from these three verses and the word is *"And God saw that it was good".*

This word was missing because the second 1000 years is a year of Noah's flood and to God it is not good. This is not a coincidence, but something known to God.

From Adam to Noah's flood is about 1656 years and that will be in the middle of second millennium. You can do the mathematics in Genesis chapter 5.

The events that took place between Genesis 6 and Genesis 8 is the period of the flood.

Genesis 6:1-8

1 And it came to pass, when men began to multiply on the face of the earth, and daughters were born unto them,

2 That the sons of God saw the daughters of men that they were fair; and they took them wives of all which they chose.

3 And the Lord said, My spirit shall not always strive with man, for that he also is flesh: yet his days shall be an hundred and twenty years.

4 There were giants in the earth in those days; and also after that, when the sons of God came in unto the daughters of men, and they bare children to them, the same became mighty men which were of old, men of renown.

5 And God saw that the wickedness of man was great in the earth, and that every imagination of the thoughts of his heart was only evil continually.

6 And it repented the Lord that he had made man on the earth, and it grieved him at his heart.

7 And the Lord said, I will destroy man whom I have created from the face of the earth; both man, and beast, and the creeping thing, and the fowls of the air; for it repenteth me that I have made them.

8 But Noah found grace in the eyes of the Lord.

In this period the fallen angels so corrupted mankind and animal that every creature except Noah and the things that were in the water were hybrid (half angel half man or half angel half animal).

This period was the beginning of witchcrafts, sorcerer, root work, science etc. All these were the secret of heaven, that the fallen angels reveal to men without the consent of God.

We can see this clearly from the book of Enoch.

THE BOOK OF ENOCH

I will take some verses from the books of Enoch as we continue, particularly about the story in Genesis 6.

Enoch6:1-8

1. And it came to pass when the children of men had multiplied that in those days were born unto them beautiful and comely daughters. 2. And the angels, the children of the heaven, saw and lusted after them, and said to one another: 'Come, let us choose us wives from among the children of men and beget us children.' 3. And Semjâzâ, who was their leader, said unto them: 'I fear ye will not indeed agree to do this deed, and I alone shall have to pay the penalty of a great sin.' 4. And they all answered him and said: 'Let us all swear an oath, and all bind ourselves by mutual imprecations not to abandon this plan but to do this thing.' 5. Then sware they all together and bound themselves by mutual imprecations upon it. 6. And they were in all two hundred; who descended in the days of Jared on the summit of Mount Hermon, and they called it Mount Hermon, because they had sworn and bound themselves by mutual imprecations upon it. 7. And these are the names of their leaders: Semjâzâ, their leader, Urâkîbarâmêêl, Kôkabîêl, Tâmîêl, Râmuêl, Dânêl, Zaqîlô, Sarâqujâl, Asâêl, Armârôs, Batraal, Anânî, Zaqêbê, Samsâvêêl, Sartarêl, Tûrêl, Jômjâêl, Arâzjâl. 8. These are their chiefs of tens, and all the others were with them.

200 angels did swear under an oath to marry women and have children.

ANGELS ARE NOT TO MARRY ACCORDING TO YESHUA.

Luke 20:34-36

34 And Yeshua answering said unto them, The children of this world marry, and are given in marriage:

35 But they which shall be accounted worthy to obtain that world, and the resurrection from the dead, neither marry, nor are given in marriage:

36 Neither can they die any more: for they are equal unto the angels; and are the children of God, being the children of the resurrection.

Yes, it is true angel are not supposed to marry, but Bible says this angel did marry and that was why God bound them because they rebel against the wish of God. Jude said they left their original state.

Jude 6

6 And the angels which kept not their first estate, but left their own habitation, he hath reserved in everlasting chains under darkness unto the judgment of the great day.

Living your original state, means change in status or transformed.

There are several cases of angels transformed to human beings in Old and New Testament and interact with men. Angels are powerful, they can transform to what they want if they choose to.

Genesis 18:2-8

2 And he lift up his eyes and looked, and, lo, three men stood by him: and when he saw them, he ran to meet them from the tent door, and bowed himself toward the ground,

3 And said, My Lord, if now I have found favour in thy sight, pass not away, I pray thee, from thy servant:

4 Let a little water, I pray you, be fetched, and wash your feet, and rest yourselves under the tree:

5 And I will fetch a morsel of bread, and comfort ye your hearts; after that ye shall pass on: for therefore are ye come to your servant. And they said, So do, as thou hast said.

6 And Abraham hastened into the tent unto Sarah, and said, Make ready quickly three measures of fine meal, knead it, and make cakes upon the hearth.

7 And Abraham ran unto the herd, and fetcht a calf tender and good, and gave it unto a young man; and he hasted to dress it.

8 And he took butter, and milk, and the calf which he had dressed, and set it before them; and he stood by them under the tree, and they did eat.

Genesis 19:1-3

1 And there came two angels to Sodom at even; and Lot sat in the gate of Sodom: and Lot seeing them rose up to meet them; and he bowed himself with his face toward the ground;

2 And he said, Behold now, my lords, turn in, I pray you, into your servant's house, and tarry all night, and wash your feet, and ye shall rise up early, and go on your ways. And they said, Nay; but we will abide in the street all night.

3 And he pressed upon them greatly; and they turned in unto him, and entered into his house; and he made them a feast, and did bake unleavened bread, and they did eat.

Angels are not supposed to eat men food either, but they can if they choose to. So, angels have free will to do what they want to do, eating does not defile, but those angels who choose to have sex defile themselves and they were punished.

Angels were described as men.

Daniel 9:21-22

21 Yea, whiles I was speaking in prayer, even the man Gabriel, whom I had seen in the vision at the beginning, being caused to fly swiftly, touched me about the time of the evening oblation.

22 And he informed me, and talked with me, and said, O Daniel, I am now come forth to give thee skill and understanding.

The book of John did not specify but I believed they were men as described in. other scriptures.

John 20:11-14

11 But Mary stood without at the sepulcher weeping: and as she wept, she stooped down, and looked into the sepulcher,

12 And seeth two angels in white sitting, the one at the head, and the other at the feet, where the body of Yeshua had lain.

13 And they say unto her, Woman, why weepest thou? She saith unto them, Because they have taken away my Lord, and I know not where they have laid him.

14 And when she had thus said, she turned herself back, and saw Yeshua standing, and knew not that it was Yeshua.

Luke called them two men.

Luke 24:4

4 And it came to pass, as they were much perplexed thereabout, behold, two men stood by them in shining garments:

Acts 1:10-11

10 And while they looked stedfastly toward heaven as he went up, behold, two men stood by them in white apparel;

11 Which also said, Ye men of Galilee, why stand ye gazing up into heaven? this same Yeshua, which is taken up from you into heaven, shall so come in like manner as ye have seen him go into heaven.

Like I said earlier Angels in their glorious state are powerful, and some have wings according to scriptures.

But when angels are seen in Scripture, they usually appear in the form of human beings, specifically as men, not as women or children.

Perhaps you too have met angels, and you don't even know it, because you were expecting to see a scary giant being with wings.

Hebrews 13:2

2 Be not forgetful to entertain strangers: for thereby some have entertained angels unawares.

maybe certain strangers who helped you in some way.

CIVILIZATION AND WITCHCRAFT

Enoch 7:1-6

1. And all the others together with them took unto themselves wives, and each chose for himself one, and they began to go in unto them and to defile themselves with them, and they taught them charms and enchantments, and the cutting of roots, and made them acquainted with plants. 2. And they became pregnant, and they bare great giants, whose height was three thousand ells: 3. Who consumed all the acquisitions of men, and when men could no longer sustain them. 4. The giants turned against them and devoured mankind. 5. And they began to sin against birds, and beasts, and reptiles, and fish, and to devour one another's flesh, and drink the blood. 6. Then the earth laid accusation against the lawless ones.

From chapter 7, we see how the fallen angels taught them enchantments and using of drugs for hallucinations so they can enter the spirit realm.

They consume all the acquisitions of men and war broke out. They commit sins with all kinds of animals too. You will notice that the women were the first to know the secret, just like Eve knew about the fruit of knowledge of good and evil before Adam.

WARFARE, SCIENCE AND ASTROLOGY.

Enoch 8:1-4

1. And Azâzêl taught men to make swords, and knives, and shields, and breastplates, and made known to them the metals(of the earth) and the art of working them, and bracelets, and ornaments, and the use of antimony, and the beautifying of the eyelids, and all kinds of costly stones, and all colouring tinctures. 2. And there arose much godlessness, and they committed fornication, and they were led astray, and became corrupt in all their ways. 3. Amêzârâk taught all the enchanters, and root-cutters, Armârôs the resolving of enchantments, Baraq'âl, (taught) astrology, Kôkabêl the signs, and Temêl taught astrology, and Asrâdêl the course of the moon. 4. And as men perished, they cried, and their cry went up to heaven.

Warfare, science and technology were also learnt in the second millennium.

ETERNAL SECRET

Enoch 9:6

6. Thou seest what Azâzêl hath done, who hath taught all unrighteousness on earth and revealed the eternal secrets which were (preserved) in heaven, which men were striving to learn:"

All the things that they taught their wives and children were eternal secrets which form the basis of witchcraft, occult science, and technology today.

But God knowledge is unsearchable, he is always ahead, he has more than what they knew. So, this is a partly knowledge of heaven.

"And as men perished, they cried, and their cry went up to heaven."

And God decided to destroy mankind (Nephilim) because they already infested and corrupt everybody but Noah and his family.

Genesis 6:5-8

5 And God saw that the wickedness of man was great in the earth, and that every imagination of the thoughts of his heart was only evil continually.

6 And it repented the Lord that he had made man on the earth, and it grieved him at his heart.

7 And the Lord said, I will destroy man whom I have created from the face of the earth; both man, and beast, and the creeping thing, and the fowls of the air; for it repenteth me that I have made them.

8 But Noah found grace in the eyes of the Lord.

WHAT HAPPENS TO THE ANGELS?

Jude 6

6 And the angels which kept not their first estate, but left their own habitation, he hath reserved in everlasting chains under darkness unto the judgment of the great day.

These angels were bound with everlasting chains in darkness. Let see the books of Enoch again.

The angels actually asked Enoch to speak to God on their behalf for forgiveness.

Enoch 13:1-5

1. And Enoch went and said: 'Azâzêl, thou shalt have no peace: a severe sentence has gone forth against thee to put thee in bonds: 2. And thou shalt not have toleration nor request granted to thee, because of the unrighteousness which thou hast taught, and because of all the works of godlessness and unrighteousness and sin which thou hast shown to men.' 3. Then I went and spoke to them all together, and they were all afraid, and fear and trembling seized them. 4. And they besought me to draw up a petition for them that they might find forgiveness, and to read their petition in the presence of the Lord of heaven. 5. For from thenceforward they could not speak (with Him) nor lift up their eyes to heaven for shame of their sins for which they had been condemned.

GOD JUDGEMENTS

Enoch 15:1-11

1. And He answered and said to me, and I heard His voice: 'Fear not, Enoch, thou righteous man and scribe of righteousness: approach hither and hear my voice. 2. And go, say to the Watchers of heaven, who have sent thee to intercede for them: "You should intercede" for men, and not men for you: 3. Wherefore have ye left the high, holy, and eternal heaven, and lain with women, and defiled yourselves with the daughters of men and taken to yourselves wives, and done like the children of earth, and begotten giants (as your) sons? 4. And though ye were holy, spiritual, living the eternal life, you have defiled yourselves with the blood of women, and have begotten (children) with the blood of flesh, and, as the children of men, have lusted after flesh and blood as those also do who die and perish. 5. Therefore have I given them wives also that they might impregnate them, and beget children by them, that thus nothing might be wanting to them on earth. 6. But you were formerly spiritual, living the eternal life, and immortal for all generations of the world. 7. And therefore I have not appointed wives for you; for as for the spiritual ones of the heaven, in heaven is their dwelling. 8. And now, the giants, who are produced from the spirits and flesh, shall be called evil spirits upon the earth, and on the earth shall be their dwelling. 9. Evil spirits have proceeded from their bodies; because they are born from men, and from the holy Watchers is their beginning and primal origin; they shall be evil spirits on earth, and evil spirits shall they be called. [10. As for the spirits of heaven, in heaven shall be their dwelling, but as for the spirits of the earth which were born upon the earth, on the earth shall be their dwelling.] 11. And the spirits of the giants afflict, oppress, destroy, attack, do battle, and work destruction on the earth, and cause trouble: they take no food, but nevertheless hunger and thirst, and cause offences. And these spirits shall rise up against the children of men and against the women, because they have proceeded from them."

God said they were not supposed to have children because they are eternal, but men were mortal, so I let them have children to carry on. As for their offspring that is the Nephilim, there spirit will become evil spirit on earth (demons) and afflicts, oppress, destroy, attack, do battle, and work destruction on earth. They shall revolt against the children of men and against women. That is exactly the works of demons today.

So, the fallen angels are not demons, they are bound with everlasting chains but the spirit of the dead Nephilim after the flood were the demons today.

Genesis 9:29

29 And all the days of Noah were nine hundred and fifty years: and he died.

Noah lived 950 years and he died and at this time the world has entered third millennium.

CHAPTER 6

DAY 3 THIRD MILLENNIUM EVENTS 2000 – 1000 BC

Third day

Genesis 1:9-13

9 And God said, Let the waters under the heaven be gathered together unto one place, and let the dry land appear: and it was so.

10 And God called the dry land Earth; and the gathering together of the waters called he Seas: and God saw that it was good.

11 And God said, Let the earth bring forth grass, the herb yielding seed, and the fruit tree yielding fruit after his kind, whose seed is in itself, upon the earth: and it was so.

12 And the earth brought forth grass, and herb yielding seed after his kind, and the tree yielding fruit, whose seed was in itself, after his kind: and God saw that it was good.

13 And the evening and the morning were the third day.

Before we continue let us know from the bible the age of the earth at the death of Noah.

The earth at the flood was about 1656 years and Noah's age at the flood is six hundred years.

Genesis 7:6

6 And Noah was six hundred years old when the flood of waters was upon the earth.

And Noah died at the age of 950 years.

Genesis 9:29

29 And all the days of Noah were nine hundred and fifty years: and he died.

So, at the death of Noah the earth was 2006 years and that was the beginning of the third millennium.

Genesis 1:9-13

9 And God said, Let the waters under the heaven be gathered together unto one place, and let the dry land appear: and it was so.

10 And God called the dry land Earth; and the gathering together of the waters called he Seas: and God saw that it was good.

11 And God said, Let the earth bring forth grass, the herb yielding seed, and the fruit tree yielding fruit after his kind, whose seed is in itself, upon the earth: and it was so.

12 And the earth brought forth grass, and herb yielding seed after his kind, and the tree yielding fruit, whose seed was in itself, after his kind: and God saw that it was good.

13 And the evening and the morning were the third day.

The third millennium was a millennium of resurgence, dry land, and vegetation. Men flourishing and fulfilling the commandment to be fruitful and multiplied. This commandment was given twice in the Bible first to Adam and second to Noah.

To Adam,

Genesis 1:28-30

28 And God blessed them, and God said unto them, Be fruitful, and multiply, and replenish the earth, and subdue it: and have dominion over the fish of the sea, and over the fowl of the air, and over every living thing that moveth upon the earth.

29 And God said, Behold, I have given you every herb bearing seed, which is upon the face of all the earth, and every tree, in the which is the fruit of a tree yielding seed; to you it shall be for meat.

30 And to every beast of the earth, and to every fowl of the air, and to every thing that creepeth upon the earth, wherein there is life, I have given every green herb for meat: and it was so.

To Noah,

Genesis 9:1-4

1 And God blessed Noah and his sons, and said unto them, Be fruitful, and multiply, and replenish the earth.

2 And the fear of you and the dread of you shall be upon every beast of the earth, and upon every fowl of the air, upon all that moveth upon the earth, and upon all the fishes of the sea; into your hand are they delivered.

3 Every moving thing that liveth shall be meat for you; even as the green herb have I given you all things.

4 But flesh with the life thereof, which is the blood thereof, shall ye not eat.

I will like you to see the different in the commandment.

To Adam it was giving to him to have dominion over the fish of the sea, and over the fowl of the air, and over every living thing that move upon the earth.

And the original diet for men and animal was herb bearing seed, which is upon the face of all the earth, and every tree, in which is the fruit of a tree yielding seed; to you it shall be for meat. So this time men are not commanded to eat meat.

But to Noah the commandment was different.

"And the fear of you and the dread of you shall be upon every beast of the earth, and upon every fowl of the air, upon all that moveth upon the earth, and upon all the fishes of the sea; into your hand are they delivered. Every moving thing that liveth shall be meat for you; even as the green herb have I given you all things."

At the time of Adam animals talk with men, which was why the serpent could talk with Eve without difficulty.

That time men don't eat animals, but men have dominion in the sense that man is superior to them and control them.

But when the fallen angels came, they turn the world upside down, they became cannibals, men started eating flesh and after the flood God did not revert it, He just commanded men not to eat blood.

And there was a striking event that took place in the third millennium which reflected Genesis 1:9.

Genesis 1:9-13

9 And God said, Let the waters under the heaven be gathered together unto one place, and let the dry land appear: and it was so.

And this event is corresponding to the parting of the red sea.

Exodus 14:21-22

21 And Moses stretched out his hand over the sea; and the Lord caused the sea to go back by a strong east wind all that night, and made the sea dry land, and the waters were divided.

22 And the children of Israel went into the midst of the sea upon the dry ground: and the waters were a wall unto them on their right hand, and on their left.

Two years after the flood the story of Abraham begin. The generation from Shem to Abraham can be found in Genesis chapter 11:10-26. From flood to Abraham departing from Ur to Canaan is 422 years. The period between Abraham call and Jacob entry to Egypt is 215 years, easily calculated from the ages of Abraham, Isaac, and Jacob.

The period spent in Egypt is 430 years according to Exodus 12:40

Exodus 12:40

40 Now the sojourning of the children of Israel, who dwelt in Egypt, was four hundred and thirty years.

480 years after leaving Egypt the first temple was built by Solomon as directed by David.

1 Kings 6:1

1 And it came to pass in the four hundred and eightieth year after the children of Israel were come out of the land of Egypt, in the fourth year of Solomon's reign over Israel, in the month Zif, which is the second month, that he began to build the house of the Lord.

From the first building unto captivity in Babylon 419 years.

Years in captivity 70 years

Period from rebuild of second temple to the coming of Yeshua HaMashiach is about 420 years. This period is called intertestamental period (Period of Silence). This time Greeks took over from Persian and Hellenize her whole empire, many things were change in this period and finally the Romans took over from Greeks.

This period the Jews were empty and thirst of words of God as God has already prophesied.

Amos 8:11-12

11 Behold, the days come, saith the Lord God, that I will send a famine in the land, not a famine of bread, nor a thirst for water, but of hearing the words of the Lord:

12 And they shall wander from sea to sea, and from the north even to the east, they shall run to and fro to seek the word of the Lord, and shall not find it.

CHAPTER 7

DAY 4 FOURTH MILLENNIUM EVENTS 1000 – 1 BC

Fourth day

Genesis 1:14-19

14 And God said, Let there be lights in the firmament of the heaven to divide the day from the night; and let them be for signs, and for seasons, and for days, and years:

15 And let them be for lights in the firmament of the heaven to give light upon the earth: and it was so.

16 And God made two great lights; the greater light to rule the day, and the lesser light to rule the night: he made the stars also.

17 And God set them in the firmament of the heaven to give light upon the earth,

18 And to rule over the day and over the night, and to divide the light from the darkness: and God saw that it was good.

19 And the evening and the morning were the fourth day.

The light again here is talking about Yeshua. The sun, moon and stars play an important role at his birth. 1000 BC David came, and it was predicted that Yeshua will come and sit on his throne forever.

Isaiah 9:6-7

6 For unto us a child is born, unto us a son is given: and the government shall be upon his shoulder: and his name shall be called Wonderful, Counsellor, The mighty God, The everlasting Father, The Prince of Peace.

7 Of the increase of his government and peace there shall be no end, upon the throne of David, and upon his kingdom, to order it, and to establish it with judgment and with justice from henceforth even for ever. The zeal of the Lord of hosts will perform this.

The Romans through Herod awaits this day and to terminate him but could not for he was taken to Egypt.

Matthew 2:1-16

1 Now when Jesus was born in Bethlehem of Judaea in the days of Herod the king, behold, there came wise men from the east to Jerusalem,

2 Saying, Where is he that is born King of the Jews? for we have seen his star in the east, and are come to worship him.

3 When Herod the king had heard these things, he was troubled, and all Jerusalem with him.

4 And when he had gathered all the chief priests and scribes of the people together, he demanded of them where Christ should be born.

5 And they said unto him, In Bethlehem of Judaea: for thus it is written by the prophet,

6 And thou Bethlehem, in the land of Juda, art not the least among the princes of Juda: for out of thee shall come a Governor, that shall rule my people Israel.

7 Then Herod, when he had privily called the wise men, enquired of them diligently what time the star appeared.

8 And he sent them to Bethlehem, and said, Go and search diligently for the young child; and when ye have found him, bring me word again, that I may come and worship him also.

9 When they had heard the king, they departed; and, lo, the star, which they saw in the east, went before them, till it came and stood over where the young child was.

10 When they saw the star, they rejoiced with exceeding great joy.

11 And when they were come into the house, they saw the young child with Mary his mother, and fell down, and worshipped him: and when they had opened their treasures, they presented unto him gifts; gold, and frankincense and myrrh.

12 And being warned of God in a dream that they should not return to Herod, they departed into their own country another way.

13 And when they were departed, behold, the angel of the Lord appeareth to Joseph in a dream, saying, Arise, and take the young child and his mother, and flee into Egypt, and be thou there until I bring thee word: for Herod will seek the young child to destroy him.

14 When he arose, he took the young child and his mother by night, and departed into Egypt:

15 And was there until the death of Herod: that it might be fulfilled which was spoken of the Lord by the prophet, saying, Out of Egypt have I called my son.

16 Then Herod, when he saw that he was mocked of the wise men, was exceeding wroth, and sent forth, and slew all the children that were in Bethlehem, and in all the coasts thereof, from two years old and under, according to the time which he had diligently inquired of the wise men.

Yeshua died and resurrected at the age of 33 years.

CHAPTER 8

DAY 5 FIFTH MILLENNIUM EVENTS 1 – 1000 AD

Fifth day.

Genesis 1:20-23

20 And God said, Let the waters bring forth abundantly the moving creature that hath life, and fowl that may fly above the earth in the open firmament of heaven.

21 And God created great whales, and every living creature that moveth, which the waters brought forth abundantly, after their kind, and every winged fowl after his kind: and God saw that it was good.

22 And God blessed them, saying, Be fruitful, and multiply, and fill the waters in the seas, and let fowl multiply in the earth.

23 And the evening and the morning were the fifth day.

In the fifth day Yahweh populate the water and the firmament.

In the fifth millennium there was population growth, knowledge increases, inventions and innovations after the death and resurrection of Yeshua.

Habakkuk 2:14

14 For the earth shall be filled with the knowledge of the glory of the Lord, as the waters cover the sea.

At the same time devil is moving faster than ever to accomplish his desire, because he has but a short time.

Revelation 12:12

12 Therefore rejoice, ye heavens, and ye that dwell in them. Woe to the inhabiters of the earth and of the sea! for the devil is come down unto you, having great wrath, because he knoweth that he hath but a short time.

This period the HOLY SPIRIT was released, and KUNDALINI at the same time was released from kingdom of darkness to counter Holy Spirit which is predominant in all churches now.

Major world religion begins to emerge and many more.

CHAPTER 9

DAY 6 SIXTH MILLENNIUM EVENTS 1000 – 2000 AD

Sith day. This is the period we are in now.

Genesis 1:24-31

24 And God said, Let the earth bring forth the living creature after his kind, cattle, and creeping thing, and beast of the earth after his kind: and it was so.

25 And God made the beast of the earth after his kind, and cattle after their kind, and every thing that creepeth upon the earth after his kind: and God saw that it was good.

26 And God said, Let us make man in our image, after our likeness: and let them have dominion over the fish of the sea, and over the fowl of the air, and over the cattle, and over all the earth, and over every creeping thing that creepeth upon the earth.

27 So God created man in his own image, in the image of God created he him; male and female created he them.

28 And God blessed them, and God said unto them, Be fruitful, and multiply, and replenish the earth, and subdue it: and have dominion over the fish of the sea, and over the fowl of the air, and over every living thing that moveth upon the earth.

29 And God said, Behold, I have given you every herb bearing seed, which is upon the face of all the earth, and every tree, in the which is the fruit of a tree yielding seed; to you it shall be for meat.

30 And to every beast of the earth, and to every fowl of the air, and to every thing that creepeth upon the earth, wherein there is life, I have given every green herb for meat: and it was so.

31 And God saw every thing that he had made, and, behold, it was very good. And the evening and the morning were the sixth day.

Day 6 animals and man were created, what does this indicated? 6 is the number of animals, 6 is the number of men, 6 is the number of the beast, as we all know that Satan was cast down as a dragon the beast. The combination of this number is 666. 666 is a warning sign of the sixth millennium, which is already manifesting on everyone.

Men were created after animal; we have seen men acting like animals for the last 1000 years.

Another thing to look at in this scripture is that everything Yahweh created were created by commandment, "let there be light", "let there be firmament", "let there be animals."

But men were created in his own image from the dust and the life which produce the blood was breath into men.

And this life and blood were made possible by the blood that was shed in the foundation of the world, so men were special to all other creatures.

Men was the last thing created on the sixth day.

The second coming of the Son of Man will be at the end of the sixth millennium. Probably 2999 plus or minus 33 years his age.

CHAPTER 10

MAN AND WOMAN

Here we will discuss the process involved in the creation of man and woman.

Unlike other things that were created through commandment, man was formed out of the dust and God breathe life into him, and he became a living soul.

Genesis 2:7

7 And the Lord God formed man of the dust of the ground and breathed into his nostrils the breath of life; and man became a living soul.

God gave man dominion over all he created.

Genesis 1:28

28 And God blessed them, and God said unto them, Be fruitful, and multiply, and replenish the earth, and subdue it: and have dominion over the fish of the sea, and over the fowl of the air, and over every living thing that moveth upon the earth.

Adam gave names to all animals.

Genesis 2:18-20

18 And the Lord God said, It is not good that the man should be alone; I will make him an help meet for him.

19 And out of the ground the Lord God formed every beast of the field, and every fowl of the air; and brought them unto Adam to see what he would call them: and whatsoever Adam called every living creature, that was the name thereof.

20 And Adam gave names to all cattle, and to the fowl of the air, and to every beast of the field; but for Adam there was not found an help meet for him.

But to him there was no companion.

Genesis 2:21-23

21 And the Lord God caused a deep sleep to fall upon Adam, and he slept: and he took one of his ribs, and closed up the flesh instead thereof;

22 And the rib, which the Lord God had taken from man, made he a woman, and brought her unto the man.

23 And Adam said, This is now bone of my bones, and flesh of my flesh: she shall be called Woman, because she was taken out of Man.

Now woman creation was a little special, she was made from ribs and flesh of Adam. She was the last thing created and she was more delicate and more beautiful.

Woman was actually created on the end of thirteenth day, hence, the reason found in Leviticus 12:1-7 for male and female purification.

Leviticus 12:1-7

1 And the Lord spake unto Moses, saying,

2 Speak unto the children of Israel, saying, If a woman have conceived seed, and born a man child: then she shall be unclean seven days; according to the days of the separation for her infirmity shall she be unclean.

3 And in the eighth day the flesh of his foreskin shall be circumcised.

4 And she shall then continue in the blood of her purifying three and thirty days; she shall touch no hallowed thing, nor come into the sanctuary, until the days of her purifying be fulfilled.

5 But if she bear a maid child, then she shall be unclean two weeks, as in her separation: and she shall continue in the blood of her purifying threescore and six days.

6 And when the days of her purifying are fulfilled, for a son, or for a daughter, she shall bring a lamb of the first year for a burnt offering, and a young pigeon, or a turtledove, for a sin offering, unto the door of the tabernacle of the congregation, unto the priest:

7 Who shall offer it before the Lord, and make an atonement for her; and she shall be cleansed from the issue of her blood. This is the law for her that hath born a male or a female.

God waited 40 days before he put Adam in the garden and 80 days before Eve was introduce unto Adam.

Adam, male 7 uncleanness + 33 purification = 40 days, Eve, female 14 uncleanness + 66 purification = 80.

Everything God created were created in ascending order of spiritual power, and descending order of physical power which put women a little higher than men in the spirit, but all this power were taken from women by Satan.

Man was to dress the garden, this implies that the earth was made without completion, but men should continue to build houses, cars, and businesses.

Genesis 2:15-17

15 And the Lord God took the man, and put him into the garden of Eden to dress it and to keep it.

16 And the Lord God commanded the man, saying, Of every tree of the garden thou mayest freely eat:

17 But of the tree of the knowledge of good and evil, thou shalt not eat of it: for in the day that thou eatest thereof thou shalt surely die.

CHAPTER 11

YEAR 2033

The second coming of the Son of Man is not known to any man, or angel according to Yeshua.

Matthew 24:36

36 But of that day and hour knoweth no man, no, not the angels of heaven, but my Father only.

But according to the 1 day to 1000 years theory we hope the son of man come at the end of the second millennium, which will be the end of the 6000 years of creation.

Many were already saying year 2000 was the end of the second millennium and nothing happens.

There will always be scoffers like in the day of Noah.

2 Peter 3:3-4

3 Knowing this first, that there shall come in the last days scoffers, walking after their own lusts,

4 And saying, Where is the promise of his coming? for since the fathers fell asleep, all things continue as they were from the beginning of the creation.

Many will not pay attention to the prophesies and warning about the last days. They will be living as if all is the same.

Luke 17:26-27

26 And as it was in the days of Noe, so shall it be also in the days of the Son of man.

27 They did eat, they drank, they married wives, they were given in marriage, until the day that Noah entered into the ark, and the flood came, and destroyed them all.

The only different between now and the day of Noah is that God is not ready to save anyone in the day of Noah but Noah and his household only, just because of the level of corruption of mankind then.

Today God does not want anyone to perish but come to repentance.

2 Peter 3:9

9 *The Lord is not slack concerning his promise, as some men count slackness; but is longsuffering to us-ward, not willing that any should perish, but that all should come to repentance.*

YEAR 2033

Actually, the second millennium will end in 2033.

The year begins it count after the death of Yeshua HaMashiach, Yeshua lived for 33 and half years.

I am not prophesying that year 2033 is the end of the world, in fact Yeshua said no one know the day or the hour but the Father.

God is supreme and does whatsoever pleases him.

Mark 13:32

32 *But of that day and that hour knoweth no man, no, not the angels which are in heaven, neither the Son, but the Father.*

But we must be vigilant and be prepared even from now for tomorrow might be too late.

Matthew 24:42-44

42 *Watch therefore: for ye know not what hour your Lord doth come.*

43 *But know this, that if the goodman of the house had known in what watch the thief would come, he would have watched, and would not have suffered his house to be broken up.*

44 *Therefore be ye also ready: for in such an hour as ye think not the Son of man cometh.*

For his coming will be like a thief in the night.

2 Peter 3:10

10 *But the day of the Lord will come as a thief in the night; in the which the heavens shall pass away with a great noise, and the elements shall melt with fervent heat, the earth also and the works that are therein shall be burned up.*

CHAPTER 12

DAY 7 THE MILLENNIUM

Seventh day, 1000 millennia reign.

Genesis 2:1-3

2 Thus the heavens and the earth were finished, and all the host of them.

2 And on the seventh day God ended his work which he had made; and he rested on the seventh day from all his work which he had made.

3 And God blessed the seventh day, and sanctified it: because that in it he had rested from all his work which God created and made.

And on the seventh day God ended his work which he had made; and he rested on the seventh day from all his work which he had made. He blessed the seventh day and sanctified it.

This is the 1000 millennia reign Bible talks about in Revelation chapter 20 and just as God rested on the 7th day these 1000 years will be a period of rest for the believers. too

Revelation 20:1-3

1 And I saw an angel come down from heaven, having the key of the bottomless pit and a great chain in his hand.

2 And he laid hold on the dragon, that old serpent, which is the Devil, and Satan, and bound him a thousand years,

3 And cast him into the bottomless pit, and shut him up, and set a seal upon him, that he should deceive the nations no more, till the thousand years should be fulfilled: and after that he must be loosed a little season.

MILLENNIUM

The elect will be caught up both dead and alive to reign with Yeshua HaMashiach in heaven for 1000 years.

The unbelievers which are not dead will continue on earth for 1000 years hopefully they will repent and make the right choice between Satan and God, which was why Satan was not send to the lake of fire yet.

THE MILLENIUM IS IN HEAVEN

Though this world is where we are all coming back to at the end of it all.

Revelation 11:15

15 And the seventh angel sounded; and there were great voices in heaven, saying, The kingdoms of this world are become the kingdoms of our Lord, and of his Christ; and he shall reign for ever and ever.

But the millennium is going to be in heaven where Yeshua has gone to prepare a place for the saints dead or alive.

John 14:1-3

1 Let not your heart be troubled: ye believe in God, believe also in me.

2 In my Father's house are many mansions: if it were not so, I would have told you. I go to prepare a place for you.

3 And if I go and prepare a place for you, I will come again, and receive you unto myself; that where I am, there ye may be also.

And for all believers' dead or alive who partook in the first resurrection.

During this period the devil will be bound, but the world will be chaotic, without order, it will be survival of the fittest for the leftover, all because of the effect the great tribulations.

Isaiah 24:1-6

1 Behold, the Lord maketh the earth empty, and maketh it waste, and turneth it upside down, and scattereth abroad the inhabitants thereof.

2 And it shall be, as with the people, so with the priest; as with the servant, so with his master; as with the maid, so with her mistress; as with the buyer, so with the seller; as with the lender, so with the borrower; as with the taker of usury, so with the giver of usury to him.

3 The land shall be utterly emptied, and utterly spoiled: for the Lord hath spoken this word.

4 The earth mourneth and fadeth away, the world languisheth and fadeth away, the haughty people of the earth do languish.

5 The earth also is defiled under the inhabitants thereof; because they have transgressed the laws, changed the ordinance, broken the everlasting covenant.

6 Therefore hath the curse devoured the earth, and they that dwell therein are desolate: therefore the inhabitants of the earth are burned, and few men left.

AFTER MILLENNIA REIGN

After millennia reign the devil will be released to further filter the leftover people in the world and take along with him to hell the remaining unbelievers, so the new world will be totally rid of evil men.

The dragon will deceive many and wage war from Gog and Magog which will be China and Russia, leaders of the final world and they will be destroyed, and the dragon will be thrown into hell fire where the beast and the false prophets are.

Revelation 20:7-10

7 And when the thousand years are expired, Satan shall be loosed out of his prison,

8 And shall go out to deceive the nations which are in the four quarters of the earth, Gog, and Magog, to gather them together to battle: the number of whom is as the sand of the sea.

9 And they went up on the breadth of the earth, and compassed the camp of the saints about, and the beloved city: and fire came down from God out of heaven, and devoured them.

10 And the devil that deceived them was cast into the lake of fire and brimstone, where the beast and the false prophet are, and shall be tormented day and night for ever and ever.

And the NEW WORLD will come.

NEW HEAVEN AND NEW EARTH

After the millennium a new heaven and a new earth will be created which will last forever. Earth is the final abode of righteous men

Isaiah 65:17

17 For, behold, I create new heavens and a new earth: and the former shall not be remembered, nor come into mind.

Isaiah 66:22

22 For as the new heavens and the new earth, which I will make, shall remain before me, saith the Lord, so shall your seed and your name remain.

2 Peter 3:13

13 Nevertheless we, according to his promise, look for new heavens and a new earth, wherein dwelleth righteousness.

Revelation 21:1-4

1 And I saw a new heaven and a new earth: for the first heaven and the first earth were passed away; and there was no more sea.

2 And I John saw the holy city, new Jerusalem, coming down from God out of heaven, prepared as a bride adorned for her husband.

3 And I heard a great voice out of heaven saying, Behold, the tabernacle of God is with men, and he will dwell with them, and they shall be his people, and God himself shall be with them, and be their God.

4 And God shall wipe away all tears from their eyes; and there shall be no more death, neither sorrow, nor crying, neither shall there be any more pain: for the former things are passed away.

The heaven will still be the abode of God and Angels and the earth will be the abode of men and Yeshua, but the barrier will be removed, and God will be worshipped unhindered.

This earth will be transformed cleansed and refreshed, the new Jerusalem will come over the old Jerusalem and a new earth will come.

Everything will be like in the garden of Eden where Adam and the animals were friendly.

GOD IS WAITING FOR YOU

God is waiting and waiting for all to repent and be saved. It is never too late to decide now.

How are we preparing in this demons and alien invested world? Turn to Yeshua, he will sustain you and set you free.

CHAPTER 13

SCIENCE AND EVOLUTION
SCIENCE

Science is called eternal knowledge and was first mention in Babylon in the book of Daniel chapter 1.

Daniel 1:3-4

3 And the king spake unto Ashpenaz the master of his eunuchs, that he should bring certain of the children of Israel, and of the king's seed, and of the princes;

4 Children in whom was no blemish, but well favoured, and skilful in all wisdom, and cunning in knowledge, and understanding science, and such as had ability in them to stand in the king's palace, and whom they might teach the learning and the tongue of the Chaldeans.

Science is a portion of heavenly knowledge revealed by the fallen angels to their human wives and hybrid children. It is the practical aspect of witchcrafts, sorcerer, astrology, magic and more. Science is the physical manifestation of all forms of witchcrafts and is the MAJOR end time tools through which the world will be controlled.

Enoch 7:1-2

1. And all the others together with them took unto themselves wives, and each chose for himself one, and they began to go in unto them and to defile themselves with them, and they taught them charms and enchantments, and the cutting of roots, and made them acquainted with plants.

That was how it all started and progressed.

Enoch 8:1-3

1. And Azâzêl taught men to make swords, and knives, and shields, and breastplates, and made known to them the metals(of the earth) and the art of working them, and bracelets, and ornaments, and the use of antimony, and the beautifying of the eyelids, and all kinds of costly stones, and all colouring tinctures. 2. And there arose much godlessness, and they committed fornication, and they were led astray, and became corrupt in all their ways. 3. Amêzârâk taught all the enchanters, and root-cutters, Armârôs the resolving of enchantments, Baraq'âl, (taught) astrology, Kôkabêl the signs, and Temêl taught astrology, and Asrâdêl the course of the moon.

It was called eternal and preserved heavenly secret.

Enoch 9:6

6. Thou seest what Azâzêl hath done, who hath taught all unrighteousness on earth and revealed the eternal secrets which were (preserved) in heaven, which men were striving to learn:"

These secrets which form the basis of science, witchcraft and occult today is a portion of heavenly knowledge. And according to Paul science has been in opposition to God and by it many have erred from the faith.

1 Timothy 6:20-21

20 O Timothy, keep that which is committed to thy trust, avoiding profane and vain babblings, and oppositions of science falsely so called:

21 Which some professing have erred concerning the faith. Grace be with thee. Amen.

Though science has being in opposition to God's knowledge for a long time, it has never been a match. The Hebrew boys at competition with the Babylonian scientist and astrologers came out ten times better.

Daniel 1:19-20

19 And the king communed with them; and among them all was found none like Daniel, Hananiah, Mishael, and Azariah: therefore stood they before the king.

20 And in all matters of wisdom and understanding, that the king enquired of them, he found them ten times better than all the magicians and astrologers that were in all his realm.

Another one can be found in Exodus chapter 7, 8, 9, 10, 11 and 12 between Moses and Pharoah. The wise men, sorcerers, and magicians of Pharaoh were able to do the same miracle with their enchantments which God commanded Moses and Aaron to perform.

They turn their rod to snakes and out of the ten plagues, they responded at least for the first two encounters (The plague of blood, and the plague of frogs). However, at the third plague when Moses and Aaron, by the power of God, brought forth lice from the sand, the magicians were not able to counterfeit this miracle. They could only exclaim, "This is the finger of God".

Exodus 8:19

19 Then the magicians said unto Pharaoh, This is the finger of God: and Pharaoh's heart was hardened, and he hearkened not unto them; as the Lord had said.

Although the magicians could turn their rods into snakes, their rods were swallowed up by Aaron's rod. Although the magicians could turn water to blood, they could not reverse the process. Although the magicians could bring forth frogs, they could not get rid of them. This shows how inferior science, magic and sorcerer were to the knowledge of Yahweh.

About the dating and year of the earth the radioactive dating said the earth is 4.5 billion and bible said the earth is 6022 years, but they forget to realize that 1 day of God can be 4.5 million years of Satan or of science and technologies.

Another thing is that the science did not put into consideration that the earth exists before man, and this can be billions years before Adam and this machine can be measuring from the day the earth was originally created.

EVOLUTION

Evolution came from Satan himself; this is Satan versus God. He is the beast that hates human that were made in the image of God.

Satan was one of YAHWEH's most beautiful creature until he fell from grace.

Isaiah 14:12-15

12 How art thou fallen from heaven, O Lucifer, son of the morning! how art thou cut down to the ground, which didst weaken the nations!

13 For thou hast said in thine heart, I will ascend into heaven, I will exalt my throne above the stars of God: I will sit also upon the mount of the congregation, in the sides of the north:

14 I will ascend above the heights of the clouds; I will be like the most High.

15 Yet thou shalt be brought down to hell, to the sides of the pit.

He was also in charge of the Eden before Adam and Eve were created to take over. Pride, greedy and desire to be like the MOST HIGH got him into deep trouble.

Ezekiel 28:12-15

12 Son of man, take up a lamentation upon the king of Tyrus, and say unto him, Thus saith the Lord God; Thou sealest up the sum, full of wisdom, and perfect in beauty.

13 Thou hast been in Eden the garden of God; every precious stone was thy covering, the sardius, topaz, and the diamond, the beryl, the onyx, and the jasper, the sapphire, the emerald, and the carbuncle, and gold: the workmanship of thy tabrets and of thy pipes was prepared in thee in the day that thou wast created.

14 Thou art the anointed cherub that covereth; and I have set thee so: thou wast upon the holy mountain of God; thou hast walked up and down in the midst of the stones of fire.

15 Thou wast perfect in thy ways from the day that thou wast created, till iniquity was found in thee.

When men were created, they were created in the IMAGE of YAHWEH.

Genesis 1:27

27 So God created man in his own image, in the image of God created he him; male and female created he them.

This coupling with many other things made him more jealous. But his desired to be worshiped was the most paramount in his heart.

At the slightest opportunity he had he collected the kingdom of the earth from men and men blessings were replaced with curses.

Genesis 3:5

5 For God doth know that in the day ye eat thereof, then your eyes shall be opened, and ye shall be as gods, knowing good and evil.

The lie of Satan is that we can become like God. But that lie was to make himself your God. The moment he gets you to sin he become your God.

And the final destination is taking men to is destruction, first he will force men to worship him by making men in his own image, the beast.

Revelation 13:16-18

16 And he causeth all, both small and great, rich and poor, free and bond, to receive a mark in their right hand, or in their foreheads:

17 And that no man might buy or sell, save he that had the mark, or the name of the beast, or the number of his name.

18 Here is wisdom. Let him that hath understanding count the number of the beast: for it is the number of a man; and his number is Six hundred threescore and six.

And secondly to end you up where he will end up.

Revelation 20:10

10 And the devil that deceived them was cast into the lake of fire and brimstone, where the beast and the false prophet are, and shall be tormented day and night for ever and ever.

Revelation 20:15

15 And whosoever was not found written in the book of life was cast into the lake of fire.

Satan hates you because you remind him of God. He wants to destroy human race. He was dethroned from perfection of beauty to dragon.

Evolution is not science is a philosophy, Satanic philosophy.

Colossians 2:8

8 Beware lest any man spoil you through philosophy and vain deceit, after the tradition of men, after the rudiments of the world, and not after Christ.

Satan want you to believe you are from him, animal and what you believe determines how you behave. If evolution is true, then.

1 Man is just an animal, a higher animal but with equal rights with animals (Animal though given equal right will always be animal).

2 Like in the jungle only the strong survive, the weakest should be eliminated (It is of the Lord mercy we the weak are not consume).

3 Superiority, one of the races of human should be superior to others and inferiors should be eliminated for the good of the species (Only Yahweh is supreme).

4 There are no absolute right or wrong (How do we decide right and wrong?).

Only God decides what is right or wrong unlike men he is faithful, and we judge through him.

FACTS about the Bible were gradually coming out through archeologist excavations, but none on evolution.

Unlike Bible evolution has no records, no written manuscript and no one has ever seen major specie evolve since creation, mutated species does not last except in viruses.

To me I think evolution if exist will be a continuous process that will not stop.

Just like God says all animals will give birth after its kinds, without manipulation so it is today. Even with modern manipulation dogs can only be breeds into variety of dogs but not into cat or goat.

And evolution has no explanation for non-living things such as the universe, planets, stars, and cosmos which according to the bible were created by God.

Psalm 8:3

3 When I consider thy heavens, the work of thy fingers, the moon and the stars, which thou hast ordained;

If anything, evolve it will be God from nothing and he created all other thing which makes him SUPREME.

CONCLUSION
PROPHECY FULFILLED
Matthew 5:18

18 For verily I say unto you, Till heaven and earth pass, one jot or one tittle shall in no wise pass from the law, till all be fulfilled.

Majority of the Bible prophecies were fulfilled accurately.

1. The promise to Abraham, also called the Land Covenant to Abraham was fulfilled. (Deuteronomy 30:1-10). Several hundred years after Abraham, Joshua led the Israelites to claim the Promised Land.

2. The promise to David. Covenant of salt. (2 Samuel 7).

God's covenant with David was that his line would never die out and that David's heir would sit on the throne of Israel forever (2 Samuel 7:16). And Yeshua is the fulfillment of this covenant.

3. The New Covenant, The Messiah. (Jeremiah 31:31-34)

The work of the New Covenant, Yeshua's death, and resurrection to reconcile hearts to God has been accomplished. But we are yet to know YESHUA HAMASHIACH the true MESSIAH.

There are still work to be done by us to overcome. It is finished but it is not yet over until the end.

THE SECOND COMING
Matthew 24:36

36 But of that day and hour knoweth no man, no, not the angels of heaven, but my Father only.

This time is coming but no one know the exact day and time, but God gave us clues about the years in his creation, we are almost there.

God can extend or shorten his time because he is God.

Matthew 24:22

22 And except those days should be shortened, there should no flesh be saved: but for the elect's sake those days shall be shortened.

There will be many prophets or Pastors that will be talking about exact time or occurrences that are happening as a sign of end time. Yeshua said this is the beginning of sorrow.

Matthew 24:5-8

5 For many shall come in my name, saying, I am Christ; and shall deceive many.

6 And ye shall hear of wars and rumours of wars: see that ye be not troubled: for all these things must come to pass, but the end is not yet.

7 For nation shall rise against nation, and kingdom against kingdom: and there shall be famines, and pestilences, and earthquakes, in divers places.

8 All these are the beginning of sorrows.

Before Yeshua can come, the world must be one and Antichrist must first come.

Matthew 24:23-24

23 Then if any man shall say unto you, Lo, here is Christ, or there; believe it not.

24 For there shall arise false Christs, and false prophets, and shall shew great signs and wonders; insomuch that, if it were possible, they shall deceive the very elect.

And the only genuine signs are what was prophesy by the Old Testament prophets and Yeshua repeated it in Mathew 24 and this is going to be after Antichrist and tribulations.

Joel 2:31

31 The sun shall be turned into darkness, and the moon into blood, before the great and terrible day of the Lord come.

Matthew 24:29-31

29 Immediately after the tribulation of those days shall the sun be darkened, and the moon shall not give her light, and the stars shall fall from heaven, and the powers of the heavens shall be shaken:

30 And then shall appear the sign of the Son of man in heaven: and then shall all the tribes of the earth mourn, and they shall see the Son of man coming in the clouds of heaven with power and great glory.

31 And he shall send his angels with a great sound of a trumpet, and they shall gather together his elect from the four winds, from one end of heaven to the other.

In this present times it seems things are normal, but not. The world is universally controlled. The WORLD WIDE WEB is a satanic device through which we are all connected.

Antichrist is already here but they are working on perfecting things and watch out and pray your way out of the MATRIX.

This is the high time to wake up.

Romans 13:11-14

11 And that, knowing the time, that now it is high time to awake out of sleep: for now is our salvation nearer than when we believed.

12 The night is far spent, the day is at hand: let us therefore cast off the works of darkness, and let us put on the armour of light.

13 Let us walk honestly, as in the day; not in rioting and drunkenness, not in chambering and wantonness, not in strife and envying.

14 But put ye on the Lord Yeshua Christ, and make not provision for the flesh, to fulfil the lusts thereof.

PRAYERS

Father in the name of Yeshua I confess that I am a sinner and I repent of my sins, and I ask that you forgive me. I confess with my mouth that Yeshua is Lord and I believe in my heart that he died for my sins and that Yahweh raised him from the dead. I declare that I will follow and serve Yeshua from now on and forever in the name of Yeshua. Amen!

Father in the name of Yeshua I renounce ZEUS, I renounce Antichrist, I renounce counterfeit Spirit, I renounce kundalini.

I repent of the sins of my ancestors in the name of Yeshua.

I repent of my sins in the name of Yeshua.

I repent of the sins of the Israelites in the name of Yeshua.

I receive forgiveness in the name of Yeshua.

I choose life in the name of Yeshua.

REFERENCES

Unless otherwise noted, all Scripture quotations
are from the King James Version of the Bible.

https://languages.oup.com/google-dictionary-en/1

https://www.bbc.co.uk/bitesize/guides/zg3vxfr/revision/1

https://www.blueletterbible.org/faq/don_stewart/
don_stewart_654.cfm

http://sites.nd.edu/james-applewhite/2020/03/22/
age-of-our-earth/

https://www.ucg.org/bible-study-tools/booklets/creation-or-
evolution-does-it-really-matter-what-you-believe/the-world-before-
man-the-biblical-explanation

https://en.wikipedia.org/wiki/Protagoras

http://jewandgreek.com/about-me/jewish-and-greek-thought/

https://en.wikipedia.org/wiki/Humanism

https://www.theguardian.com/us-news/2017/sep/20/end-of-
white-christian-america

https://www.imb.org/2019/02/11/empty-churches-europe/

https://www.independent.co.uk/news/uk/atheists-countries-list-
six-world-most-convinced-a6946291.html

https://www.quora.com/What-percentage-of-the-universe-does-
earth-take-up

https://people.howstuffworks.com/books-of-bible.htm

https://en.wikipedia.org/wiki/Biblical_canon

https://en.wikipedia.org/wiki/Chronology_of_the_Bible

About the Author

ABOUT THE AUTHOR: Joshua Olumoye is the founder and Pastor of Harmony Heavenly Church a fellowship of genuine believers of Yeshua HaMashiach. He authored more than twenty books, including *For his glory, Far superior host, Far superior weapons,* and the best-selling books *Russia and China leads in end time.* With the ability to rightly dividing the word through grace of God, he easily brings out the truth of the mystery of the bible.